7/3/84

To Pat

With Warmest Personal Regards

Cynthia
Jerry

# The
# Art
# of
# Shrinking

# The Art of Shrinking

poems by *Jerome J. Klinman, M.D.*
drawings by *Cynthia S. Klinman, Ph.D.*

𝟘
Argent Press
New York

THE ART OF SHRINKING

1 2 3 4 5 6 7 8 9

Library of Congress Catalog Card Number: 83-73313
ISBN 0-915417-00-6

# Contents

## The Art of Being a Therapist — 43

## The Art of Being Off Duty — 95

## The Art of Being a Patient

## The Art of Terminating Therapy

# The Art
## of
# Becoming a Therapist

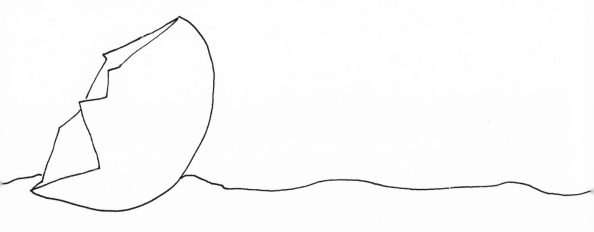

# STRESS INTERVIEW

At the Psychiatric Center
Dr. Diddle sat in fear.
Would he qualify to enter
As a resident this year?
He knew well the reputation
Of the famous Institute
And he hoped, with trepidation,
That they'd make him a recruit.
They had answered every question
And had shown him every floor.
Now he sat with indigestion
Outside Dr. Schmartz's door.
Oh, this psychiatric giant
Was a legend, Diddle knew,
So he'd try to be compliant
In the coming interview.
With a flourish and a swagger,
Dr. Schmartz called Diddle in.
Diddle tried hard not to stagger
Or to show his nervous grin.
"Please be seated, Dr. Diddle."
Sit down where? poor Diddle thought.
In this chair here in the middle?
Diddle felt a bit distraught.
Or that far chair near the curtain?
No, he'll think I'm too remote.
Why am I so darned uncertain?
Diddle coughed and cleared his throat.

Maybe I should sit a little
Closer to the doctor there.
Oh, my, no! thought Dr. Diddle.
He will notice my despair.
"You seem anxious," said the master.
Dr. Diddle stifled: Ouch!
Felt his heart race faster, faster—
Plopped down on the doctor's couch.
"How's it going?" Schmartz inquired.
Diddle smiled, "Fine, so far."
Schmartz glanced up as if inspired
As he reached for a cigar.
"You said, 'Fine, *so far*,'" he stated.
"You're expecting problems here?"
Diddle thought, I've been checkmated
In the opening, I fear.
Diddle said, "I've heard it rumored
That your questions create stress."
Diddle prayed, Please be good-humored,
Get me out of this big mess.
"So you thought I'd do some poking."
Schmartz seemed somewhat titillated.
His cigar he kept on smoking
And the stench poor Diddle hated.

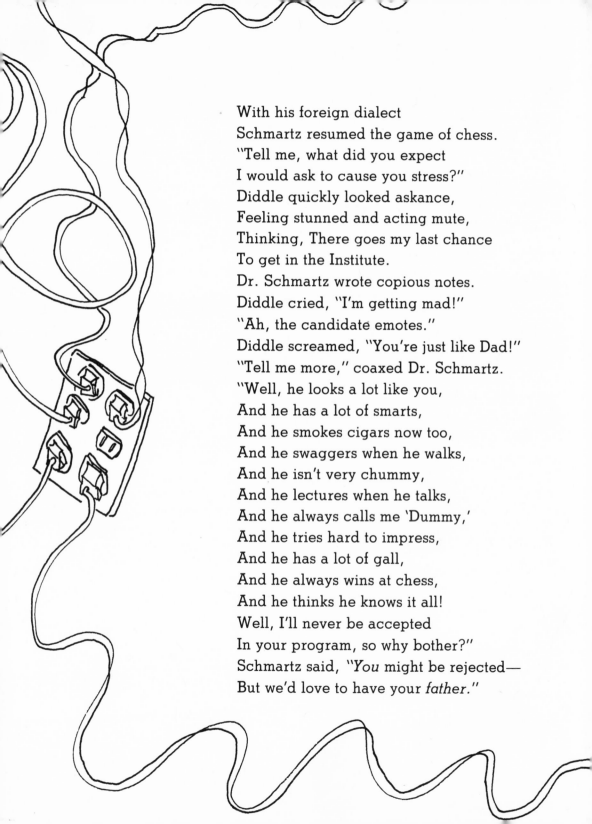

With his foreign dialect
Schmartz resumed the game of chess.
"Tell me, what did you expect
I would ask to cause you stress?"
Diddle quickly looked askance,
Feeling stunned and acting mute,
Thinking, There goes my last chance
To get in the Institute.
Dr. Schmartz wrote copious notes.
Diddle cried, "I'm getting mad!"
"Ah, the candidate emotes."
Diddle screamed, "You're just like Dad!"
"Tell me more," coaxed Dr. Schmartz.
"Well, he looks a lot like you,
And he has a lot of smarts,
And he smokes cigars now too,
And he swaggers when he walks,
And he isn't very chummy,
And he lectures when he talks,
And he always calls me 'Dummy,'
And he tries hard to impress,
And he has a lot of gall,
And he always wins at chess,
And he thinks he knows it all!
Well, I'll never be accepted
In your program, so why bother?"
Schmartz said, "*You* might be rejected—
But we'd love to have your *father*."

# FRUSTRATION TOLERANCE

Diddle waited for the mail
Every day, to no avail.
Would the letter never come?
Was the Center keeping mum?
He knew what he most expected:
Tough luck, Diddle, you're rejected!
Diddle groaned, "I'd be destroyed.
Better pray to Sigmund Freud."

One day through his letter chute,
Something from the Institute!
Diddle's hands were shaking mildly,
Diddle's heart was thumping wildly.
Every dream and hope in it.
Should he dare to open it?
Held his breath and peeked inside.
"This can't be!" poor Diddle cried.
"Give me YES or give me NO,
Give me COME or give me GO.
Something tangible to tempt me,
Not an envelope that's . . . empty!"

Diddle phoned the Institute,
Heard a voice say, "That's a beaut!
You must speak to Dr. Schmartz.
These decisions he imparts.
He's away, though, I should mention—
An emergency convention.
Will the wait be hard to bear?
Dr. Diddle . . . Are you there?"

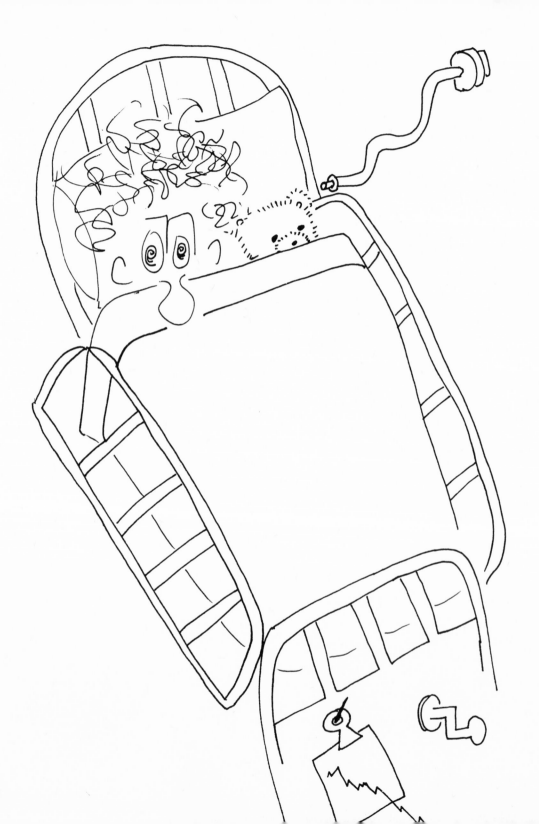

## FIRST PATIENT

"Won't my lack of skills surprise her?"
Diddle asked his supervisor.
"I'm not certain what to say.
Does she know it's my first day?
I need something to rehearse.
I'm afraid I'll make her worse.
I don't think it's very kind
Having patients here assigned
When we're grossly unprepared.
Frankly, sir, I'm very scared.
Is her mental state contageous?
This is totally outrageous!
Oh, this hurdle's too gigantic.
What if she is schizophrantic!
How can I look dignified
When I want to run and hide?
I can hear the others laugh,
'He's a *doctor* on the staff?'
Will I be the first to enter
As a doctor at the Center
And discover I must stay
As a *patient* my first day?"

## NEW BEARD

Dr. Diddle, it looks weird.
I'm referring to your beard.
Is the stubble just implying
That you are identifying
With your famous counterparts,
Dr. Freud and Dr. Schmartz?
Since that fuzzy thing you grew,
I'm not certain you are you.
And I'm currently deciding
Whether it means you are hiding.
But don't think you're so disguised
That you won't be recognized.
We'll still spot you on the street, so
Don't assume you're incognito.

How can anyone mature
If his shrink is insecure?

## PERCHANCE TO SLEEP

"Diddle!" the professor barked.
"You've been sleeping in my class.
That's a zero I have marked.
How do you expect to pass?
This is an important course:
'Dream Interpretation Two.'
It could be a fine resource
In the therapy you do.
Your behavior's not in keeping
With the standards of the Center.
Do you think, son, that by sleeping
You'll endear this poor old mentor?"

"My behavior is in keeping
With the *course*," said Diddle, beaming.
"Sir, it's not that I was sleeping—
But the fact that I was dreaming."

## C-C-CORRECT ANSWER

"Diddle!" the professor shot.
"Tell us about stuttering."
Diddle woke up. "W-W-What?"
They all heard him uttering.

## AT FIRST BLUSH

"Diddle! Try to be effectual!
Tell the class what causes blushing."
Diddle squeaked, "The cause is sexual,"
As he felt his cheeks start flushing.

## NURSES' STATION

Diddle, aching with frustration,
Slumped inside the nurses' station,
Upping all the medication,
    Feeling dizzy, seeing double.
Not one patient was remitting.
Diddle felt his temples splitting.
He was on the verge of quitting
    When a nurse asked, "What's the trouble?"
Diddle screamed, "No one gets well!
This profession's really hell!
If I knew a magic spell,
    Then, perhaps, I'd see a cure!"
She sighed, "Doctor, such dismay.
Magic spells are not the way.
Their prognosis is OK—
    *Yours,* however, seems unsure. . . ."

## SHRINK THINKS

My Shrink thinks I'm terrific;
He thinks it more and more.
My Shrink won't be specific.
He's hedging I am sure.

My Shrink thinks I'm delightful;
I have him in my spell.
My Shrink, I think, is frightful.
He doesn't know me well.

My Shrink thinks I'm a winner;
He's thought it all along.
My Shrink is a beginner.
How could he be so wrong?

My Shrink thinks I'm progressing;
He's just a resident.
My Shrink thinks it's distressing
That I'm not president.

My Shrink thinks I'm the greatest;
He's acting very odd.
And have you heard the latest?
My Shrink thinks *he* is God.

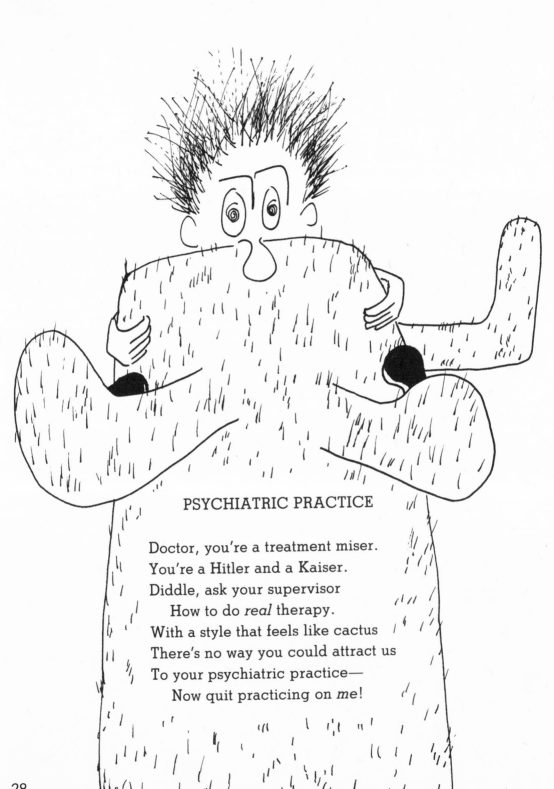

## PSYCHIATRIC PRACTICE

Doctor, you're a treatment miser.
You're a Hitler and a Kaiser.
Diddle, ask your supervisor
   How to do *real* therapy.
With a style that feels like cactus
There's no way you could attract us
To your psychiatric practice—
   Now quit practicing on *me*!

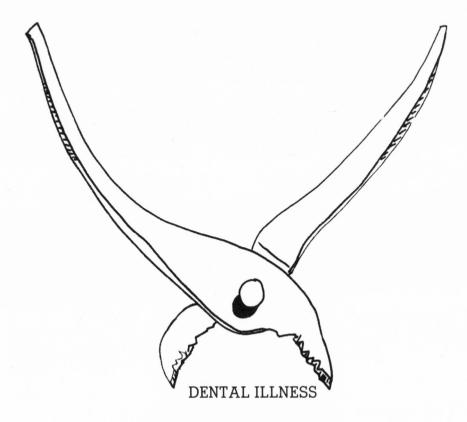

DENTAL ILLNESS

"Isn't that a new degree?
It says 'D.D.S.,' I think.
Doesn't that mean 'Dentistry'?
What's that for, Doc? You're a Shrink.
Furthermore," the patient noted,
"Isn't this a dentist's chair?"
Dr. Diddle sat and gloated,
Pleased his patient was aware.
Diddle said, "My work is stressing
Getting to what's underneath.
Dentistry may prove a blessing
When my job's like pulling teeth."

## FLAMING PINK

Furnishing his office was
Something Diddle came to hate.
Time passed quickly, as it does,
And his furniture was late.
A new patient would be coming
At a quarter after four.
Diddle found his fingers strumming
On the empty office floor.
Suddenly he heard his bell,
And his pulse raced just a little.
Then he heard a workman yell,
"Someone here named Dr. Diddle?"
In they brought a garish desk,
Not the one that he had chosen.
Diddle thought it looked grotesque
And he stood there feeling frozen.
Next they carried in some chairs.
One of them was badly torn,
Others needed some repairs,
All looked just a trifle worn.
Diddle watched the men unpack
His new couch, then raised a stink.
"I selected 'Rorschach Black'—
You have brought me 'Flaming Pink'!"
"What you get is what you see,"
Shrugged the workman. "Sign in ink."
"How can I do therapy
With a couch of 'Flaming Pink'?

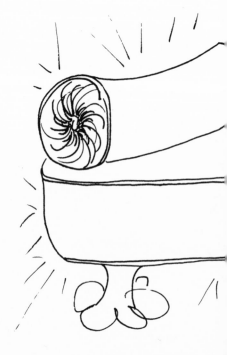

What a total nightmare, this!
What will my new patients think?
Who can do analysis
On a couch of 'Flaming Pink'?"
When he let his patient in,
Diddle's heart began to sink
For he saw her gape and grin
At the couch of "Flaming Pink."
"Doctor, my main problem is
Furnishing my place anew,
But I see *you're* no great wiz.
I'm much better off than you!"
"Doctor, you are so appealing,"
Cooed the next one with a wink,
As she gazed with fervent feeling
At his face of "Flaming Pink."

## CLINK

Doc, I hate this therapy!—CLINK
        And I hate your guts!—CLINK
That you make us pay your fee—CLINK
        This way, Doc, is nuts!—CLINK
Doc, I really hate your gall!—CLINK
        Even Scrooge is sweeter!—CLINK
But what I hate most of all—CLINK
        Is this crazy METER!—CLINK

# ARCTIC WHITE

When the men came late that morning
With the carpet and the pad,
Dr. Diddle had no warning
That again he had been had.
"This could drive a doctor loco!"
Diddle's voice was full of fight.
"I had ordered 'Desert Cocoa'—
You have brought me 'Arctic White'!"
"It don't come in that there color
Anymore." The tone was mean.
"Would've made your office duller,
And white's easier to clean."
As they carpeted in white,
Diddle felt quite skeptical.
Covered everything in sight,
Even the receptacle.

His first patient spilled a little
Coffee on that pristine fleece.
After that, poor Dr. Diddle
Didn't have a moment's peace.
Oh, the anguish and defiance,
The frustration and disgust,
For his city-dwelling clients
Brought in tar and grime and dust,
Cigarette and cigar ashes,
Bubble gum from someone's shoe,
Dripping blood from cuts and gashes,
Mud and slush and doggy do.
"My good fortune," Diddle dubbed it,
"That white's easier to clean."
As it was he scrubbed and scrubbed it
Night and day . . . and in between.

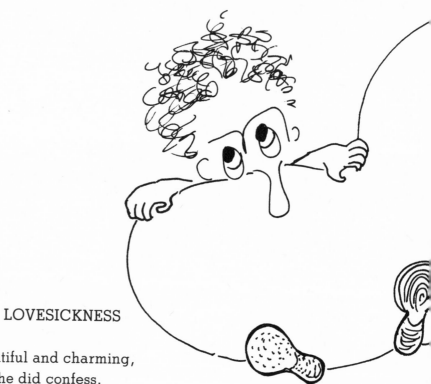

## LOVESICKNESS

She is beautiful and charming,
To himself he did confess.
And she's totally disarming—
But "my patient" nonetheless.
She was tender and appealing
And as gentle as a dove.
How he reveled in the feeling!
Dr. Diddle was in love.
He had heard that this could happen
Yet he'd felt he was immune.
Now his heart was clearly tappin'
Out a sweet romantic tune.
He was dazzled by the vision
Of her loveliness and grace.
He rejoiced in her decision
To stop dating for a space.

He arranged to see her often
And he charged her very little.
He could feel his insides soften
When her voice breathed, "Dr. Diddle."
He'd begin their sessions early
And would tend to keep her late.
She became a special girl he
Started treating like a date.
She reminded him of Betty,
His first love in grammar school,
For his legs felt like spaghetti
And he acted like a fool.
When his Betty had ignored him
Diddle pined for days and days.
All the other girls had bored him
With their superficial ways.
This sweet patient, just like Betty,
Had become a fantasy,
And he recognized this, yet he
Blotted out reality.
She began to do quite poorly
And she suffered visibly.
He felt dreadful, for this surely
Was not helpful therapy.
So he told her of his feeling
Then referred her to a friend,
And she quickly started healing
While he thought *he'd* never mend.
Diddle's patients coyly smiled
As his heart began to patch,
For his eyes looked far less wild
And his shoes began to match.

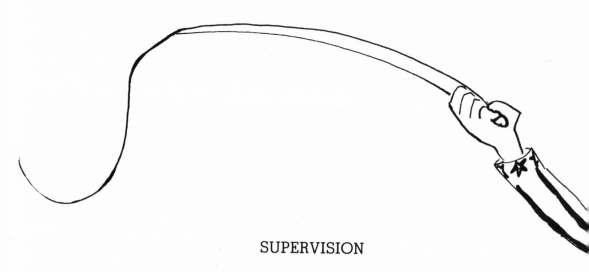

## SUPERVISION

"Supervision is confusing,"
Moaned the resident that day.
"Good!" smiled Diddle. "Stop refusing
To examine what I say."
"But you say I'm so efficient
That I don't make a mistake.
I try hard to be proficient.
What is wrong, for goodness' sake?"
"Nothing," Diddle answered cooly.
"That's your problem you've been told.
Nothing's ruffled or unruly,
Everything is too controlled.
*Just don't try so hard!* Your ardor
Keeps your work from being greater."
"Thank you, Doctor. *I'll try harder.*"
"Good!" beamed Diddle. "See you later."

# EXPERT WITNESS

"In your role as expert witness,
Dr. Diddle, please explain
If there's psychiatric fitness
Or this person is insane."
It was Diddle's first appearance
As a witness in the court
And he asked the judge for clearance
To present his long report.
"He has schizoid-like relations
And his affect is quite flat.
There are loose associations . . ."
Diddle rambled on like that.
With a swagger and a flourish,
The next witness looked so grand.
Diddle thought that he would perish—
Dr. Schmartz stood on the stand!
Dr. Schmartz, his old professor
And his *analyst,* to boot!
Sigmund Schmartz—the Great Assessor
From the famous Institute!

"Well, my colleague, Dr. Diddle,
Calls this gentleman insane.
Please forgive him. He's a little
Bit inept, if not inane.
Your report is too redundant,
Your analysis is lax,
And your jargon's too abundant,
And you don't support your facts,
And you call this man a 'crazy'?
Well, I've interviewed him too.
In your work here you've been lazy—
He is healthier than you!
For he doesn't bite his nails,
And he doesn't tease his brother,
And he never, never fails
To call home each week to mother,
And he doesn't pick his head,
And he doesn't gobble pills,
And he doesn't wet the bed,
And he pays his doctor bills!"
"I am guilty, Sir, Your Honor,"
Diddle blurted tearfully.
"And I fear I am a goner
But I plead 'insanity.'
I will sign a full confession,
But before my sentence starts,
May I keep my evening session
With the famous Dr. Schmartz?"

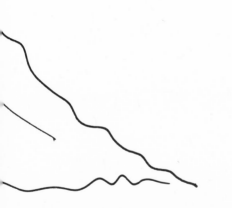

# The Art
# of
# Being a Therapist

## SILENCE

"I'm not thinking! It's a bore!"
　　Silence filled the room with dread. . . .
"I'm not talking! That's the score!"
　　Silence heavier than lead. . . .
"I'm not coming anymore!"
　　Silence as if one were dead. . . .
"I'm not paying! That's for sure!"
　　"What was that?" the doctor said.

# PSYCHOPHARMACOLOGY

"Dr. Diddle! Dr. Diddle!
Won't you be a little doll
And prescribe for me a little
Of that phenobarbital?"
    "I am sorry to refuse you,"
    Diddle said decisively,
    "But such pills would just confuse you.
    What you need is therapy."
"Dr. Diddle, I'm so nervous,
And the reason that I come
Is in hopes you'll do a service
And prescribe some Valium."
    "I regret I must frustrate you
    By withholding medication,
    But it only would sedate you.
    Let's consider meditation."
"Dr. Diddle, my depression
Needs some pills to intervene.
Won't you kindly use our session
To prescribe amphetamine?"
    "Once again I must deny you
    Any drugs," the doctor said.
    "I am thinking that I'll try you
    On hypnosis here instead."
"Dr. Diddle, you're frustrating!
You will drive me off my bean!
I am now hallucinating.
You must give me Thorazine!"

"Why do patients have to bug me?
It becomes a test of wills.
They say, 'Dope me up and drug me.'
But I rarely give them pills."
"Dr. Diddle! You're a cynic
And I think that you're a quack!
I am going to the Clinic
And I'm never coming back!"
She departed like a rocket!
Diddle felt upset and numb,
So he reached into his pocket
For a dose of Librium.

$50

At the closing of the hour
Dr. Diddle left his chair,
But Miss Grumble, looking sour,
Just continued sitting there.
"Will you lend me fifty dollars?"
Grumble groused. "I've not a dime."
Diddle thought, What would the scholars
Say to Grumble at this time?
"Session's over," Diddle told her
And approached the office door.
Peering back behind his shoulder,
He saw Grumble as before.
"I'm not leaving empty-handed,"
Grumble grumbled very low.
Diddle gulped, "That's very candid,
But you really have to go.
Other patients will be coming,
You must leave this room at once!"
But Miss Grumble sat there humming,
And she hadn't hummed in months.

Diddle warned, "I'll have to move you.
I am tougher than I seem."
Grumble growled, "It would behoove you
To desist or I will scream!"
Diddle tugged her by the ankles
And he pulled her by the hair.
Grumble screamed a scream that rankles . . .
And held tightly to the chair.
Diddle held his other sessions
In the waiting room that day.
(There are four or five regressions
And a lawsuit under way.)
Still Miss Grumble sat demurely,
Getting stronger by the sec.
Dr. Diddle, doing poorly,
Was a psychiatric wreck.
Diddle thought, I'll call the Center.
What an awful scandal, this!
I must speak to my old mentor.
Dr. Schmartz could handle this.
Schmartz intoned, "Don't bust your collar!
It's so easy, don't you see?
Simply lend her fifty dollars—
And send fifty more to me."

# THE SCARY IRS

He had half expected "GREETINGS"
When he first received the letter.
After seven separate readings,
He thought "greetings" would be better.
Diddle struggled with the tension;
When the panic came he fought it.
Did the notice really mention
He was scheduled for an AUDIT?
His accountant he had dialed
But found out he was in jail.
Then his troubles really piled
And his hopes began to fail,
For he tried to reach his lawyer
But his lawyer wouldn't phone.
He must face this great destroyer
And must face it all alone.
Held the meeting with a fellow
From the scary IRS,
And his insides turned to Jell-O
But he stifled: "I confess."
Diddle offered Chivas Regal
Or some coffee to imbibe.
"Don't you know it is illegal
Tempting me with such a bribe!"
Diddle cried, "I'm not inflicting
Any sort of bribes on you."
"Now you're into contradicting. . . .
That, I think, we'll call 'Strike Two'!"

Diddle asked, "What is the reason
For this audit? It's a blow."
"Well, your question smacks of treason
But you have a right to know.
I believe you're a physician.
Doctors cheat, it would appear.
Are you also a musician?
'Metronome' you list right here."
"Oh, I use that in my practice
For hypnosis," Diddle stated.
"It works quickly and the fact is
Deeper sleep can be created."
Diddle flipped the lever gently,
Thinking, Now's my only chance.
And the agent stared intently
Till he fell into a trance.
Dr. Diddle merely swallowed
When the agent left—and, yes,
Quite a hefty refund followed
From the scary IRS.

## THE CAUSE OF MENTAL ILLNESS

"Doctor, your name does remind me
Of a classmate in first grade.
He would sneak up close behind me . . .
Now with men I am afraid.
He would tease about my glasses,
His assaults were episodic,
And he'd mock me in our classes—
*He's* the reason I'm neurotic!
He was always so pathetic
Trying to be teacher's pet.
He was dumb and unathletic.
I recall his nickname yet:
'Dippy Diddle' we all called him
'Cause he had such dippy ways
And that nickname sure appalled him,
He would cry and sulk for days.
But it's strange I can't remember,"
Mused the patient, deep in doubt,
"Who the teacher was . . ." "MISS DEMBER,"
Dr. Diddle blurted out.

## INSURANCE

Diddle looked with great abhorrence
At the forms of health insurance.
It was trying his endurance,
　　All this paper work!
And what made it more dismaying
Was the slowness of their paying;
Months and months of such delaying,
　　Thought he'd go berserk!

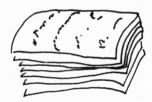

So he played a little game:
Wrote in "Freud" for DOCTOR'S NAME.
It would really be a shame
  If this form they'd shun.
SEX became "Hermaphrodite,"
RACE, of course, was "Arctic White."
"Giant" he put down for HEIGHT.
  This was really fun!
What to write for DIAGNOSIS?
Not "Anxiety neurosis."
Why not "Mental halitosis"?
  Yes, that sounded right.
TREATMENT PLAN was "Chlorophyll,"
For PROGNOSIS he wrote "Nil,"
CHARGES were "Eleven mill."
  This was out of sight!
Now to fill in his DEGREE.
Not, of course, the old "M.D."
He wrote "Third" real casually
  On that silly page.
Sent the form that very day
Knowing they would never pay.
They returned it right away—
  "Fill in patient's AGE."

# TICK, TOCK

TICK, TOCK, TICK, TOCK,
    50 minutes on my clock.
    My, he thinks he's quite a jock!
TICK, TOCK, TICK, TOCK.

TICK, TOCK, TICK, TOCK,
    40 minutes on my clock.
    What a baby! What a crock!
TICK, TOCK, TICK, TOCK.

TICK, TOCK, TICK, TOCK,
    30 minutes on my clock.
    His defense is like a rock!
TICK, TOCK, TICK, TOCK.

TICK, TOCK, TICK, TOCK,
    20 minutes on my clock.
    What this infant needs is shock!
TICK, TOCK, TICK, TOCK.

TICK, TOCK, TICK, TOCK,
    10 more minutes on my clock.
    Did I hear the next one knock?
TICK, TOCK, TICK, TOCK.

TICK, TOCK, TICK, TOCK,
    1 more minute on my clock.
    I'll refer this one to Spock!
TICK, TOCK, TICK, TOCK.

# PATIENT INTERRUPTUS

The patient droned, "There was no other,
Only me and my young brother
And of course my darling mother—
    And do you know what she said?"
At that moment something crashed,
Then the door burst open, smashed.
In he barged—his dagger flashed.
    "One fast move and you're both dead!"
The burglar entered with a knife.
"Don't move, buddy, or your wife!
It's your money or your life!
    Give me all your dough and drugs!"
Diddle leaped up from his seat.
(What he screamed we won't repeat.)
He would not take this defeat,
    Couldn't stand these brazen thugs!
Diddle rammed him with his head.
"OOF!" the startled robber said.
Down the blade slashed—Diddle bled
    But he gave the brute a slug.
The mugger's skull crashed on the desk
(Which no longer looked grotesque).
Diddle did an arabesque
    And then slumped upon the rug.
The thief just lay there in a heap.
The gash he suffered had been deep.
Diddle sat there half asleep
    Feeling sore in every sinew.
His aching body felt like lead,
His carpet now had spots of red. . . .
"Do you know what my mother said?"
    He heard someone there continue.

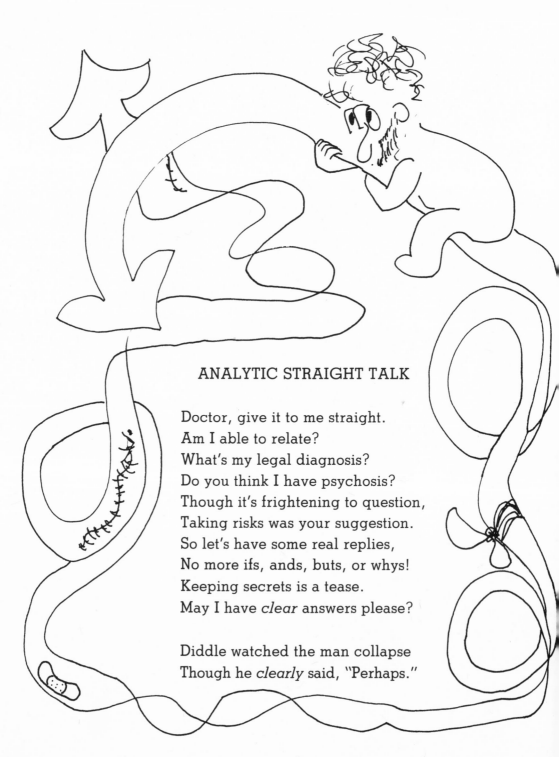

## ANALYTIC STRAIGHT TALK

Doctor, give it to me straight.
Am I able to relate?
What's my legal diagnosis?
Do you think I have psychosis?
Though it's frightening to question,
Taking risks was your suggestion.
So let's have some real replies,
No more ifs, ands, buts, or whys!
Keeping secrets is a tease.
May I have *clear* answers please?

Diddle watched the man collapse
Though he *clearly* said, "Perhaps."

# MUSIC THERAPY

I thought my doctor didn't speak
So he could muse about each word,
A psychological technique
To contemplate all that he heard.
While on the couch I turned around
To see him muse at what I'd said.
I watched him contemplate each sound
From Walkman earphones on his head.

# EVERYBODY'S HERO

You're everybody's hero,
You're worshipped and adored.
But I feel like a zero.
I'm totally ignored.

You're everybody's guru,
Your patients all agree.
But all the magic you do
Just isn't helping *me*.

You're everybody's savior,
You act just like a saint.
But look at *my* behavior.
An angel I just ain't.

You're everybody's prophet,
They've given you a crown.
But I wish you would doff it
And from your throne come down.

You're everybody's idol,
High on a pedestal.
But I feel homicidal.
Perhaps it's Oedipal.

They keep you much too busy.
I'd like to tell a few,
"He's not *your* Daddy, is he?
I need him more than you."

# ONE-NIGHT STAND

"Doctor, it is out of hand.
I wonder if I wear a brand
Which labels me a 'one-night stand.'
    Upon my heart this problem weighs.
I'll have a new and super date,
Then by my phone I'll wait and wait
Because I'm sure I heard him state,
    'I'll call you in a couple days.'
Of course he never calls again.
This whole thing is beyond my ken.
I don't know if it's me or men.
    Upon my mind this problem plays.
I'll meet a man and dig his style.
We're intimate in just a while.
'We must arrange a date,' he'll smile.
    'I'll call you in a couple days.'
But, naturally, he is afraid,
Or maybe I don't make the grade.
I desperately would like your aid.
    Upon my soul this problem preys."
The doctor spoke with some mystique,
"Your problem isn't too unique.
We must arrange a time each week—
    I'll call you in a couple days."

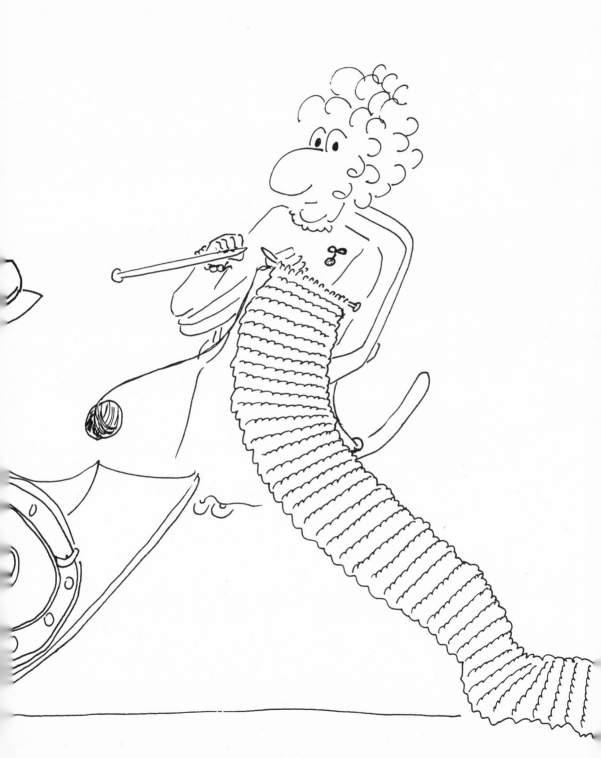

## ADDICTION

Yes, young man, you are afflicted,
We might even say "addicted,"
Not to alcohol or pot,
Though you dig those drugs a lot,
But to all of those machines
That destroy you in your teens:
Pac-Man, Frogger, Lost Ark Raiders.
Will our youth become Darth Vaders?
I've heard you miss lots of school
Playing Asteroids and pool.
Don't you know that if you're truant
Your whole life will soon be ruin't?

Oh, your teacher needs advice?
Wants to see me once or twice?
I've no time to see her, sorry—
I just got a new Atari.

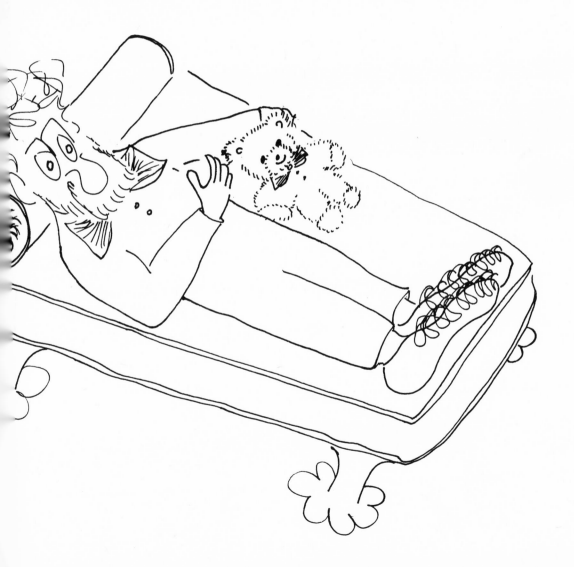

## MOVIE STAR

"A celebrity you are."
Diddle stared at shoes by Gucci.
"You're my favorite movie star,
Next to Bogart and Belushi.
We must never let your fame
Interfere with therapy.
You'll be treated just the same
As the others that I see."
When that made his patient smirk
Diddle gave a little laugh
And said, "Sir, before we work,
May I have your autograph?"

# NOT ANGRY

"I'm not angry," smiled the shrink.
"What could ever make you think
I'd be ruffled or annoyed?
Don't you know that's anti-Freud?
I'm not angry. That's a fact,
Even though at times you act
Heartless and insensitive—
My mistakes you won't forgive.
I'm not prone to feeling rages
Though you haven't paid in ages
And you call each night at four
And drop ashes on my floor.
I'm not angry!" screamed the shrink,
"Even though you spatter ink
On my carpet and my chair—
Though I do confess I care.
I'm not angry!" shrieked the shrink,
"Though I may be on the brink
When you swear you'll institute
Quite a large malpractice suit.
I'm not angry," Diddle sniffed.
"Maybe just a trifle miffed."

## ZZZzzzz

The doctor wakened with a start.
His patient was about to weep.
"Last week you doodled in my chart,
Today you fall asleep!"
The doctor straightened out his tie
As if to smooth his dignity.
"Of course," he preached, "you wonder why
I'm dozing openly.
I haven't mentioned this before,"
The doctor held forth with a frown,
"But you are somewhat of a bore."
He set his meerschaum down.

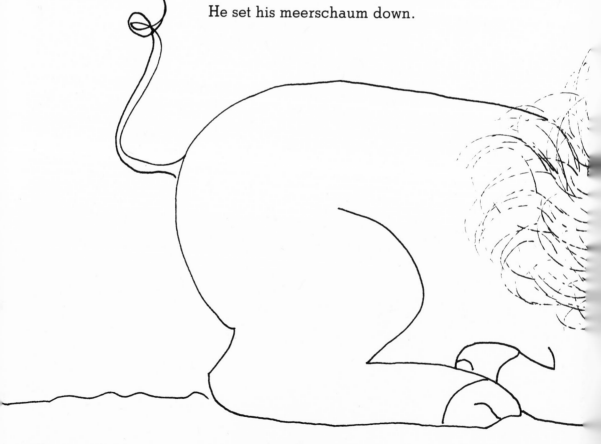

"You always tend to talk or cry
Or chatter on without surcease.
You never give the other guy
A chance to say his piece.
And if you tend to ramble here,"
(Each syllable was slowly stressed)
"You ramble everywhere, I fear."
The doctor looked impressed.
His insights tumbled, one, two, three.
How fortunate that he had snoozed!
How glorious this therapy!
Interpretations oozed.
"Besides, I had a wondrous dream,"
The doctor lectured with a grin.
"Unconscious going at full steam."
He stroked his bearded chin.
"I dreamt of a ferocious beast.
I can't remember too much more.
The symbolism's there, at least;
I'm sure it was a BOAR."
The office echoed everywhere
His lofty words so rich and deep.
No answer from the other chair—
The patient lay asleep. . . .

# PLAY THERAPY

"Dr. Diddle, you're in check."
Diddle gasped and craned his neck.
Little Skip, who just turned eight,
Grinned, "This session's really great!
Playing chess with you is neat!"
Diddle squirmed upon his seat.
He was treating little Skip
Mainly for poor sportsmanship.
Little Skip was a bad loser,
An abuser and accuser.
Any time he didn't win,
Temper tantrums would begin.
Dr. Diddle thought he'd play
Chess with little Skip that day
And when Skip's game bit the dust,
He would help the child adjust.
But poor Diddle wasn't winning
And that tiny twerp was grinning.
He could beat a child of eight!
Moved his King and heard, "Checkmate!"
Diddle shrieked, "You little brat!
How did you maneuver that?
You're too little to defeat me!
I suspect you tried to cheat me!
And your grinning is bizarre!
What a rotten sport you are!"
Little Skip said, "Don't be mad,
Losing isn't all that bad.
It is just a game, you see.
Maybe next week you'll beat me."

# HICKORY, DICKORY, DOC

"I'm Dr. Diddle. I treat big and little.
What brings you here this noon?"
    "Hey, Dr. Diddle, the cad with the fiddle,
    The kid jumped over the moon."
"I have been told you're eleven years old
And speak only nursery rhymes,
And your conversation gives much irritation
To people who hear you sometimes."
    "Simple Diddle met a kiddle
    Going to the fair.
    Said Simple Diddle to the kiddle,
    'See my underwear.'"
"That is evasive and hardly persuasive,"
Said Diddle. "So why won't you try?"
    "Diddle, piddle, pudding and pie,
    Treats the kids and makes them cry."
"If you are sad, my fine little lad,"
Said Diddle, "let's see how you tick."
    "Jake be nimble, Jake be quick,
    Jake jump over the patient's shtick."

"I'm not overjoyed to see you avoid
Speaking normally here with me now.
I think you're afraid of the contact we've made.
Proper dialogue you won't allow."

    "Little Jake Diddle sat on the griddle,
    Eating a pompous pie;
    He took a big bite, pulled out an insight,
    And said, 'What a good Doc am I!"

"You are too much and I feel out of touch,"
Groaned Diddle, upset and uptight.
"How can we speak to each other each week,
If you will not talk to me right?"

    "Humpty Diddle put up a wall,
    Humpty Diddle had a great fall;
    All the king's horses and all the king's carts
    Cannot get Diddle to old Dr. Schmartz."

"Hickory, Dickory, Doc!"
Raved Diddle, unnerved and in shock.
"The clock's striking one, our session is done.
Mother Goose, I'll be joining your flock!"

## RUBIK'S SYNDROME

"Dr. Diddle, I'm obsessed.
I just feel like such a boob.
I am totally regressed
Playing with this Rubik's Cube.
Doctor, this preoccupation
Makes our session a disaster.
There's no free association,
Only 'corner twirls' to master.
Doc, my future's growing bleaker.
I can't lie here too much longer,
For my psyche's growing weaker
Though my wrist is growing stronger.
Save me from this vile affliction!
Rubik's Syndrome's what I've got.
If I'm plagued with an addiction,
Why not something cool, like pot?
Was my oral stage upsetting?
Was my anal stage a blast?
Is there something I'm forgetting
From my dark unconcious past?"
"THAT'S IT!" Diddle's outburst shocked her.
"At last!" Diddle's patient cried.
"Have you a solution, Doctor?"
"Yes—I have the whole blue side!"

# THE ECONOMICS OF THERAPY

"Yes, you claimed your stock would soar, sir,
And it flew up out of sight.
Up a hundred points or more, sir,"
Diddle grinned, "and you were right."
Then the doctor, calmly seated,
Said, "You don't enjoy your gain.
You're still sullen and defeated,
Steeped in anguish, wracked with pain.
Feelings just aren't in control, sir,
That's the thing we can't abide.
Clear perspective is our goal, sir,
Even if that stock should slide.
Oh? You say the stock is falling?
That you sold it yesterday?
That your broker had been calling
And you dumped it right away?
What? You say the stock is CRASHING?
Dropped 300 points by noon?
And you pity those not cashing
In, as you did, very soon?
What? You say I'm agitated?
Feelings just aren't in control?
And you say you are persuaded
That I've left the 'doctor's role'?
Well, I can't take stock right now, sir,
Can't take stock right now at all.
I must stop the clock right now, sir—
Got to make an urgent call!"

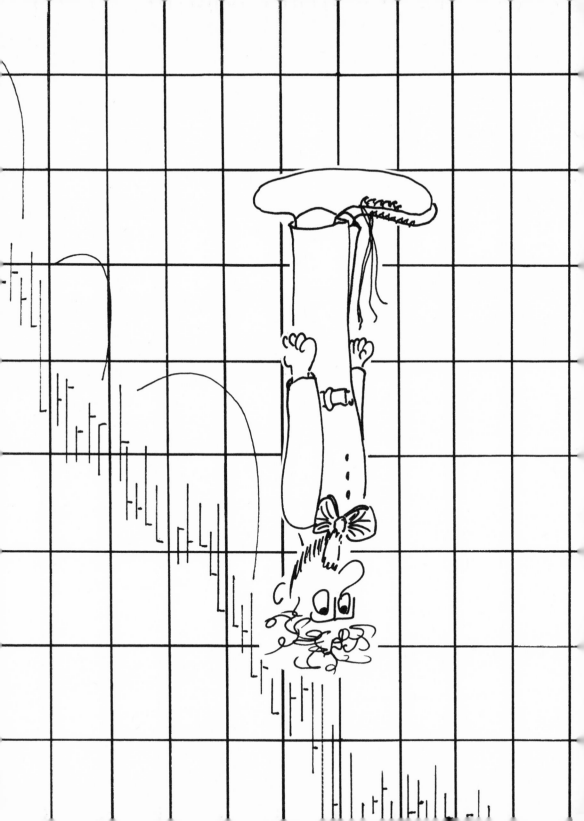

# FEARS

"Dr. Diddle, I am ailing.
You must hear of my distress,
For I have a fear of failing
Which has hindered my success."
 Diddle smiled, "You've made an error
 That I think we should amend.
 It's *success* that brings you terror,
 Failure's been a lifelong friend."
"Dr. Diddle, though I'm only
Twenty-three, I'm out of phase.
I'm afraid of being lonely
For the balance of my days."
 Diddle answered, "There's no danger
 Any panic will appear.
 Loneliness has been no stranger,
 *Intimacy* is the fear."
"Dr. Diddle, I've been crying.
In my head there is such pain.
I am petrified of dying
From a growth inside my brain."
 Diddle soothed, "You think of cancer
 When you feel anxiety.
 Fear of dying's not the answer,
 Fear of *living* is the key."
"Dr. Diddle, you have shown me
How my thinking is askew.
Please explain how this may hone me
Into someone brave like you."
 Diddle smiled, "You've comprehended
 And your question's very keen.
 But . . . I fear our session's ended."
"Fear of *questions*, Doc, you mean!"

## THE ANALYST'S VIEW

"From this couch I cannot see you
Sitting in your comfy chair,
And I wonder can it be you,
Or is someone different there
Like my father or my mother—
Is this totally distortion?
Like my sister or my brother—
Is reality a portion?
And I wonder what you're doing,
Since I think, and it's been ages,
That there's something you are viewing,
For I hear you turning pages."

"You must hear the notes I'm writing,"
Diddle gulped. "Your hearing's keen."
And he hid his new exciting
Sexy *Playboy* magazine.

## THERE, THERE, MY DEAR

Doctor, please be sympathetic,
I've been coming for a year.
Make me strong and energetic,
Say the words I need to hear:
    There, there, my dear, my dear.
    There, there, my dear.

Doctor, please be understanding,
Pamper me, but be sincere.
Keep my worries from expanding,
Breathe the words I long to hear:
    There, there, my dear, my dear.
    There, there, my dear.

Doctor, you're so cold and distant
When I want you to be near.
Why must you be so resistant?
Speak the words I have to hear:
    There, there, my dear, my dear.
    There, there, my dear.

Doctor, I'm a nervous wreck now,
And our session's done, I fear.
I could write you out a check now
If there were a pen in here.

    "THERE! THERE! My dear, my dear.
    THERE! THERE! My dear."

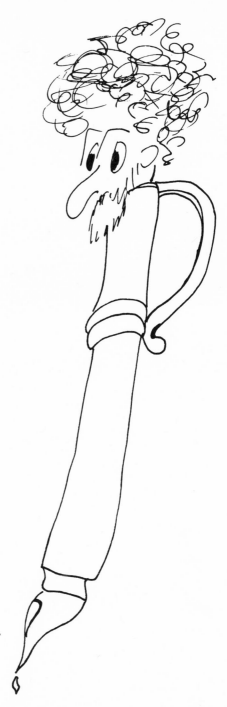

# INFLATION

"I regret I must inform you
That my fees are due to rise."
Dr. Diddle watched the storm brew
In his patient's angry eyes.
"What, again!" the patient blustered.
"Surely this must be a joke!
I am slowly getting flustered
And I'm swiftly going broke!"
Diddle sighed, "I hate to do it
But the cost of living's soared.
If you're strapped we can review it
To see what hike you'll afford."
"Well, you know my business foundered,
And you've heard about my stock,
And my real estate has floundered.
I might have to go in hock.
And I'm paying alimony,
And my gambling debts are high,
And the gems I bought were phony,
And my rent is to the sky.
They may cancel my insurance,
And my yacht's about to sink.
I am poor beyond endurance.
Tell me, Doctor, what you think."
Ah, such smooth manipulating,
And he'd played it to the hilt,
Then he sat there calmly waiting
While his doctor sparred with guilt.
Dr. Diddle could intuit
Much about that cunning plea,
But before he even knew it . . .
He'd reduced the *present* fee.

## COUPLES THERAPY

Diddle washed and dressed that morning,
Went downstairs to have his tea.
Heard an outburst without warning,
"How damned selfish can you be?"
"What?" asked Diddle of his wife.
She screamed, "Playing dumb, of course!
You're the cause of all my strife—
And I'm thinking of divorce!"
"Huh?" winced Diddle, stupified.
"Please explain, what did I do?"
"You're an idiot!" she cried.
"You forgot to make the stew!"
"But that's *your* fault," Diddle started.
"You were saying just last night . . ."
Out the door she quickly darted,
Out of earshot, out of sight.

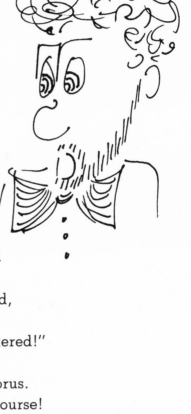

To his office Diddle staggered,
Just as upset as could be.
He was feeling much too haggard
To do Couples Therapy.
When the troubled couple entered,
She seemed bitter and irate.
"You are just so damned self-centered!"
She yelled shrilly at her mate.
"What?" both men asked as a chorus.
She snarled, "Playing dumb, of course!
You're the cause of all my tsuris—
And I'm thinking of divorce!"
"Huh?" the timid man asserted.
"Please explain, what have I done?"
"You're an idiot!" she blurted.
"You forgot to toast my bun!"
"But that's *your* fault!" Diddle socked her.
"You were saying just last night . . ."
"We were not here last night, Doctor—
Are you sure that you're all right?"

## BEAR IT

In the Group the patient said,
"God, I wish that I were dead!
I have trod where one can't tread."
Then her face turned blazing red.

Diddle spoke encouragingly,
"You must share it and be free.
Here we deal in honesty.
You will bear it. So will we."

"After last week's Group," she started,
"I found after we'd departed,
That my purse I had discarded,
So back to this room I darted.
Opening the door with care,
I saw Diddle sleeping there.
He was in his underwear. . . .
CUDDLING A TEDDY BEAR."

Diddle's face turned blazing red.
She had trod where one can't tread.
God, he wished that she were dead!
"Group dismissed," poor Diddle said.

# REJECTION

"Doctor, give me some direction.
I am tortured by rejection.
Do you know that kind of pain?
I'm afraid I'll go insane.
I've been searching for a mate
But can't even get a date.
This pain festers, never heals.
Oh, how bad rejection feels!
I am trapped in an abyss.
Have you ever felt like this?"

"Yes," groaned Diddle. "Even worse!
Have you tried to publish verse?"

# SCHNOCKERED

Dr. Diddle had a little drink before the Group tonight.
Thought no one would notice that he wasn't feeling right.

Dr. Diddle tried to fiddle with his watch alarm tonight.
Thought no one would notice that the beeps were not polite.

Dr. Diddle told a riddle to impress the Group tonight.
Thought no one would notice that it sounded rather trite.

Dr. Diddle did belittle someone in the Group tonight.
Thought no one would notice that he did it out of spite.

Dr. Diddle had to piddle halfway through the Group tonight.
Thought no one would notice that he clamped his knees real tight.

Dr. Diddle saw some spittle on his left lapel tonight.
Thought no one would notice that he tucked it out of sight.

Dr. Diddle saw the middle of the office spin tonight.
Thought no one would notice that he clung with all his might.

Dr. Diddle felt quite brittle as the Group disbursed tonight.
Hoped no one had noticed that he was a little tight.

## GROUCH ON THE COUCH

The patient sat in Diddle's chair
While Diddle lay upon the couch.
The patient fussed, "This isn't fair!"
The doctor snapped, "You're such a grouch!"
The patient grinned, "But Freud would say
You really didn't have his knack."
The doctor groaned, "But in his day
He really didn't have my back."

# The Art
## of
# Being Off Duty

# ORGY

Dr. Diddle groped in darkness,
Sat down in the second row.
Didn't mind the theater's starkness,
Had to see this evening's show.
Ate his Jujy Fruits completely,
Chomped on bagels stuffed with lox,
Nibbled M & M's discreetly,
Dipped into the popcorn box.
What an orgy! What regression!
Far from nagging patients' calls.
What a cure for his depression!
Started on the sour balls.

Someone several rows behind him
Squealed, "That's him! Oh, what a scoop!"
Why did that voice so remind him
Of a patient in his Group?
"That's not him," another muttered.
"That's not HIM! How could that be?"
"Oh, m-my g-goodness," Diddle stuttered.
"What's become of privacy?
Could I be hallucinating?
Oh, if that were only true!
This is too humiliating.
What am I supposed to do?"
"If that's Diddle, he's a sickie!"
He heard yet another say.
"Watching this dumb porno flick, he's
Diddling the night away!"
Diddle thought, Oh, what a blunder!
I need more than Coke to drink.
What will all my patients wonder?
What will all my colleagues think?
Do they know it's me for certain?
Is it dark enough in here?
Should I hide behind the curtain?
Could I simply disappear?
Hey, what's happened to the voices?
Why, my patients slipped away!
Did they exercise their choices
And decide they shouldn't stay?
I've just got to be more cautious.
That was quite a narrow squeak!
All that popcorn made me nauseous. . . .
Say, what's playing here next week? _____  _____

## PHYSICAL THERAPY

Diddle's back went into spasm
So he joined the local gym.
Went there with enthusiasm,
Thought he even might get trim.
Donned his brand new workout shirt,
Flexed his arm and cocked his thumb,
Puffed his chest out till it hurt.
"Watch out, Arnold, here I come!"
Slid beneath the Universal.
As a dolt he was the best!
Should have asked for a rehearsal—
Down it crashed across his chest!
Why the mechanism jammed,
The attendant might have known.
All he said was, "I'll be damned!"
Then went chatting on the phone.
Diddle struggled to get free,
Cursed and screamed inside the gym,
Flailed about hysterically . . .
No one came to rescue him.

Suddenly across the room
He heard someone's voice he knew.
Diddle gagged—A voice of doom.
"Dr. Diddle! Is that you?"
Down she sat upon his thigh,
An old patient from the past.
"I'm so glad that you dropped by,
I can talk to you, at last.
Did you know my mother died?"
Said the woman as a starter.
Then she wailed and sobbed and cried.
Dr. Diddle floundered harder.
"When I couldn't pay the rent,
That mean landlord kicked me out.
Every penny I have spent,
And my brother got the gout."
Diddle clenched his teeth in fury.
How he struggled to get free!
He could kill her, and the jury
Would acquit him instantly.
Dr. Schmartz, he realized,
Would know how to end this pain.
His advice he fantasized:
Exhale, Dummy! Use your brain!
Diddle squirmed out, nearly retching.
Good thing that his head was small.
Left the woman and her kvetching,
Hid inside a shower stall.
He sneaked home in poor condition
When it got to be quite late.
Gave up dreams of competition,
"Mr. Universe" must wait.

## MOUTH TO MOUTH

After quitting at the gym,
Diddle thought, Well, I can swim.
So he joined a fancy club,
Went there eager as a cub,
Got into his bathing suit,
Gave the lifeguard a salute,
Grabbed a towel and diving mask,
Found a sunny spot to bask.
Now, at last, some privacy!
And some anonymity!
Suddenly across the way,
Thought he heard the lifeguard say,
"Yes, Miss Treadwell, warm as soup."
Not Miss Treadwell from his Group!
Thought he'd better hide his face,
Put the diving mask in place,
Slumped down in his lounging chair. . . .
"Dr. Diddle!" filled the air.
She continued, "*You're* a member?
I've been coming since December.
I'm still in the shallow pool.
I should join the swimming school.
Oh my goodness! You're so cute
In your bright pink bathing suit,
And you've hair upon your chest!
Bet you've passed *your* swimming test!"
Underneath the mask he wore,
Sweat streamed out of every pore.
Diddle leaped up from his chair—
Patients! Patients! Everywhere!

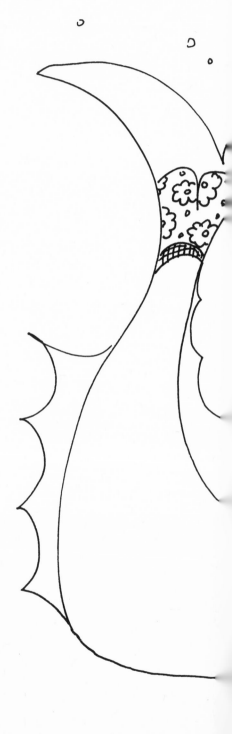

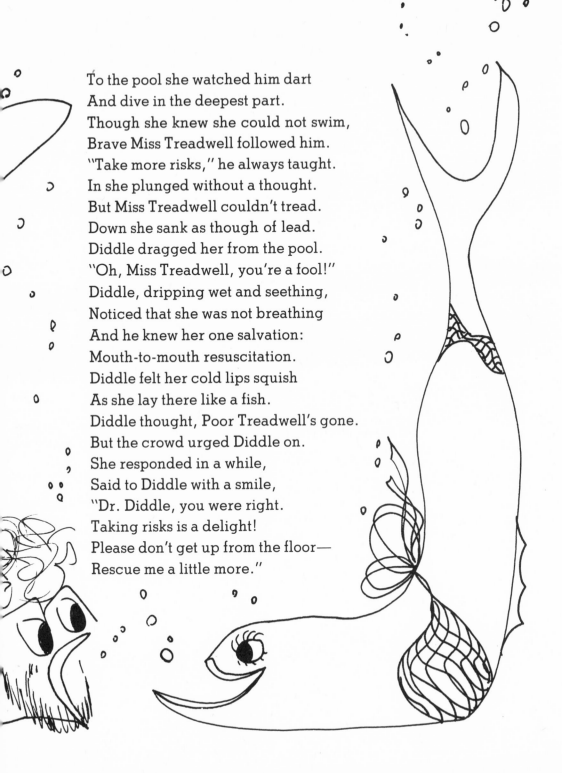

To the pool she watched him dart
And dive in the deepest part.
Though she knew she could not swim,
Brave Miss Treadwell followed him.
"Take more risks," he always taught.
In she plunged without a thought.
But Miss Treadwell couldn't tread.
Down she sank as though of lead.
Diddle dragged her from the pool.
"Oh, Miss Treadwell, you're a fool!"
Diddle, dripping wet and seething,
Noticed that she was not breathing
And he knew her one salvation:
Mouth-to-mouth resuscitation.
Diddle felt her cold lips squish
As she lay there like a fish.
Diddle thought, Poor Treadwell's gone.
But the crowd urged Diddle on.
She responded in a while,
Said to Diddle with a smile,
"Dr. Diddle, you were right.
Taking risks is a delight!
Please don't get up from the floor—
Rescue me a little more."

## AEROBIC THERAPY

"This will surely soothe my psyche!"
Diddle stretched a little more
As he double-tied his Nike
At the crowded reservoir.
He had jogged but fifty meters
When his knee began to hurt.
"Can't keep up with all these speeders
With the numerals on their shirt."
He was struggling and panting,
But his head was feeling clear
When he heard a woman ranting
Several meters to the rear.
Diddle started feeling moody.
"This could turn out a disaster.
Thank the stars I am off duty!"
Diddle sprinted slightly faster.
"Doctor, I am feeling brittle!"
He heard someone calling loud.
He felt queasy in his middle
As he mingled with the crowd.
"Dr. Diddle! Dr. Diddle!"
He heard someone scream his name.
He had jogged right off the griddle
And had dashed into the flame.
In his misery he wallowed.
He was wondering if Freud
Also felt that he was followed.
Was he getting paranoid?

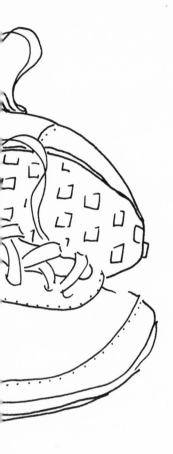

"Dr. Diddle! Dr. Diddle!"
Now the voice was very close.
He was feeling just a little
Bit unsettled and morose.
She caught up and looked quite nervous,
Just a jogging ball of fear.
"I called up and reached your service,
And they told me you were here."
"Oh, my service! Oh, my service!"
Diddle shrieked into the air.
"I don't think that I deserve this!"
Diddle bordered on despair.
"I have read," he heard her mention,
"Jogging sometimes helps depression.
Since I'm feeling all this tension,
Could we have a 'running session'?"
Trapped and tired, Diddle stumbled
Round and round and round the park.
On and on the patient mumbled
Till the sky grew very dark.
Diddle started getting shin splints
And his skin began to crawl
And his brain was seeing imprints
When he finally "hit the wall."
Though his patient felt elation,
Diddle felt tremendous blues.
While she burned with admiration,
Diddle burned his running shoes.

## DANCE THERAPY

At the ballet Dr. Diddle
Watched enchanted and impressed.
Sitting downstairs in the middle,
In his best suit he was dressed.
All the greats he came to see:
Tcherkassky and Baryshnikov,
Bujones and Ms. Gregory,
Makarova and Godunov.
What a marvelous vacation
Just to have an evening free,
And he gazed in admiration
At the choreography.

Suddenly his beeper sounded—
That meant an emergency!
All the patrons who surrounded
Diddle shushed him angrily.
What a time for a malfunction!
Couldn't turn the damned thing off!
Had to leave with some compunction.
He could hear them hiss and cough.
Exiting was simply awful
From the center of the row.
Someone whispered, "It's unlawful
To disturb this splendid show."
Hostile patrons fussed and pouted
That this clod should make a scene.
"Dr. Diddle!" someone shouted
Just then from the mezzanine.
"That's my DOCTOR! There's some trouble!
Don't you hear those beeps?" he cried.
"Let him exit on the double!
It may be—a SUICIDE!"
Diddle, mortified and stewing,
Tried to find a working phone.
"If a suicide is brewing,
It will surely be my own!"

## APPETITE SUPPRESSANT

They were chopping, they were slicing,
They were shredding, they were dicing,
The aromas were enticing
    At the Chinese Cooking Course.
Dr. Diddle hummed in class.
They were making Hunan Bass.
Clean the wok! Ignite the gas!

    He was hungry as a horse.
Little did he know there'd lurk
Someone who would go berserk,
Interrupting all their work

    As they deftly minced the ginger.
When she threatened with a cleaver,
Half the class did not believe her.
Not that pleasant Mrs. Reever!

    What could ever so unhinge her?
"Call a cop!" screamed out the teacher.
"She's become a wild creature!
Just a miracle can reach her."

    "I'm a DOCTOR!" shook the room.
Dr. Diddle volunteered.
All his classmates cheered and cheered.
Mrs. Reever neatly sheared
    Fifteen inches off a broom.

"Mrs. Reever, please be calm."
Diddle soothed her like a balm.
Then he offered her his palm.

"You're no doctor!" Reever said.
"Doctors take anatomy.
You can't carve as well as me!
You should take Psychiatry."

Diddle took the blade instead.
Reever shouted, "I've been robbed!"
Then she turned away and sobbed.
Diddle's heartbeats really throbbed

As the police came into sight.
While the class enjoyed the feed—
Hot and spicy, they agreed—
Diddle didn't eat, for he'd

Somehow lost his appetite.

# WITHDRAWAL

It was over half an hour
But his turn was coming next.
"Slow bank lines can make you sour,"
Diddle muttered, feeling vexed.
"Dr. Diddle! Just the person!"
Mr. Silver looked quite grim.
Diddle squelched some ugly cursin'
As his patient stood with him.
"You barged in because I know you,"
Diddle fussed.  "That's not polite."
"Fifteen dollars I still owe you,"
Silver blushed. "I'll pay tonight."
Silver lifted up his collar,
Put a mask upon his face,
Told the teller, "Fifteen dollars!"
Then dashed quickly from the place.
Even though the hold-up shocked her,
The bank teller, mystified,
Asked, "Who was that masked man, Doctor?"
"HI HO SILVER!" Diddle cried.

# RECREATIONAL THERAPY

At the Chess Club, Diddle wondered
What move he'd be making next.
His opponent clearly blundered,
Which left Diddle quite perplexed.
Should he capture with his King Pawn
Or the Bishop or the Rook?
What revenge would these moves bring on?
Diddle felt a little shook.
Once he'd make this timely capture
Then his triumph would begin.
Ah, the ecstacy and rapture
Thinking he at last might win!
After weeks and weeks of playing,
He had hardly won a game.
"Potzer" he heard people saying
At the mention of his name.
"Dr. Diddle! Dr. Diddle!"
Someone mentioned it just then.
The poor doctor gasped a little,
"Oh, it's happening again!"
To his table, without warning,
Came his patient, lacking grace.
"I just joined the club this morning.
Good to see a friendly face.
How're you doing? Are you winning?
You must be the champion here!
This game's only just beginning
And he's lost, it would appear."

Dr. Diddle writhed in fury,
Knocked the chess clock to the floor.
All his fantasies were gory,
He was raging to the core.
"Watch his Knight retaliation,"
Coached his patient, ill at ease.
Diddle reached in pure frustration—
And his Queen he placed *en prise*. . . .
"Bobby Fischer you are not, sir,"
Sneered the patient, rather vexed.
"Gads, to think my shrink's a potzer.
Diddle—will you play *me* next?"

# SUPERSHRINK

Schmartz asked, "Why is it upsetting?"
Diddle blurted, "You're forgetting
That to be the most effective
Psychological detective
I must be a plain blank screen,
Never known and hardly seen,
And to get to their libido
I must function incognito.
Each encounter, each occurrence,
Interferes with the transference."
Schmartz said, "Outside when you're caught,
Underneath you're overwrought.
And, of course, when I meet you
Outside . . . I should tremble too."
"No!" snapped Diddle. "That's not right.
I don't see you get uptight."
"Well," shrugged Schmartz, "what do you think?"
Diddle cried, "You're SUPERSHRINK!
And it's rescuing I need
With a speeding bullet's speed.
In my role as therapist,
Anxious feelings I resist.
But outside I feel so shy,
Patients spot me and I die.
Is this coming from my past?"
Diddle had the thought, at last.

He left hopeful, stepped outside. . . .
"Dr. Diddle!" someone cried.
Diddle froze and clutched his chest.
"I'm not ready for a test!"
Sneaked into a phone booth there—
Patients! Patients! Everywhere!
And the phone booth made him think,
Hurry, save me, SUPERSHRINK!

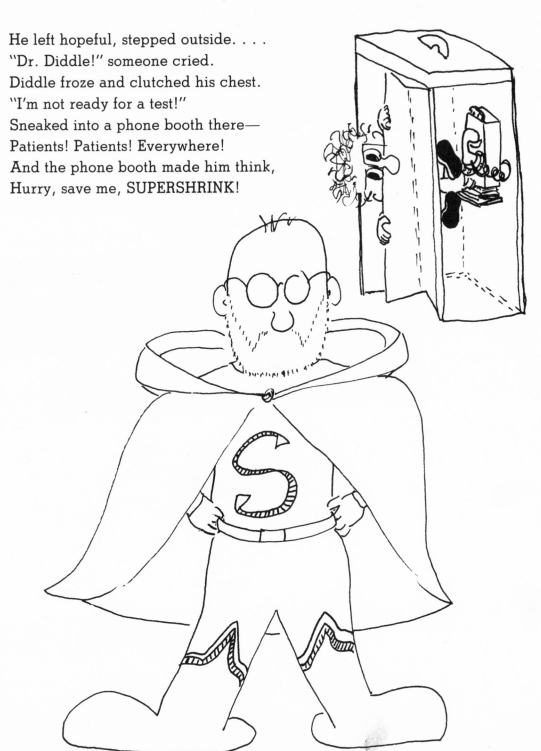

# VACATION

Dr. Diddle was excited—
A vacation in a week!
You could tell he was delighted,
    He could barely speak.
Should have told his patients sooner.
Such poor planning! How absurd!
Now to face each grand harpooner
    As he spread the word.
Mr. Alkie started drinking,
Mrs. Lumox got depressed,
Charles showed some concrete thinking,
    Gwendolyn regressed.
Little Herbie was arrested
On a charge of sodomy,
Mr. Winkleman requested
    A lobotomy.
Jennifer was so ecstatic,
"I'll save all that bread!" she cried.
Mrs. Gombie burned the attic,
    Seven people died.

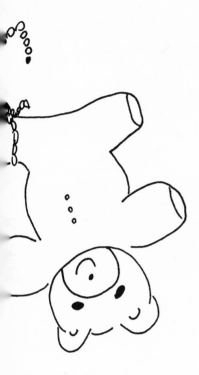

Mr. Dole spent all his savings
On a trip around the globe,
Mr. Peeps revealed his cravings
    Flashing in his robe.
Wednesday's Group had quite an orgy,
Stoned on acid, pot and beer.
Friday's Group hung crazy Georgie
    From the chandelier.
Mr. Twizzle quit his business
Just to have a little fun.
Mrs. Twizzle shrieked, "What is this?"
    And she bought a gun.
Rosemarie, his anorectic,
Started dieting for sure,
Mr. Gog went apoplectic
    And could speak no more.
Suicide was mentioned often,
Homicide was mentioned too.
Mrs. Cackles bought a coffin.
    What should Diddle do?
Diddle called for an appointment
With the famous Dr. Schmartz,
Whose advice was like an ointment:
    "Show me all their charts."
All his patients Schmartz then treated.
Diddle flew away quite grim,
Thinking they would all feel cheated
    To return to him.

## IN A STEW

"I will plan a good safari,"
Spoke the hunter anxiously.
"But it's surely hari-kari
In this jungle, you will see.
There are pygmies in the brush
And fierce cannibals survive.
Why are you in such a rush
To be eaten up alive?"
"I am followed everywhere
By my patients," Diddle said.
"But there's no one who would dare
To pursue me where I'll head."
So they trudged for many miles
Through the jungle dark and damp,
Fighting snakes and crocodiles,
Chasing lions from their camp.
Then one night—catastrophe!
Blow guns spewing poisoned darts.
Diddle, all alone, ran free
Screaming, "Save me, Dr. Schmartz!
Where are all my patients now?"
Diddle wailed into the night.
"It's ironic to me how
No one spots me in this plight."
He was spotted near the pillage
By some cannibals—a lot.
And was taken to their village
Where they plunked him in a pot.

As they stoked the blazing fire
And they stirred their tasty brew,
Diddle screamed, "This funeral pyre
Will make bitter Diddle stew!"
"Diddle stew?" came back an echo.
"Did I hear a 'Diddle' stew?"
The witch doctor craned his neck—"Oh,
Dr. Diddle! Is that you?"
"Dr. Bush?" asked Diddle straining.
"My old roommate in *this* mob,
After 15 years of training?"
Bush shrugged feebly, "It's a job."
So they chewed a little fat
And they swapped some dirty jokes
And they spoke of this and that
And they talked about their folks.
Diddle chuckled, "I've been thinking
That your work must be such fun.
You are into *real* 'head shrinking'!"
Bush cracked up at Diddle's pun.
Diddle sighed, "I have to go.
Hope I haven't been much trouble."
Left the caldron all aglow
Just as it began to bubble.
Bush said, "I neglect my studies,
Keep me current in the arts.
Give my best to all our buddies,
Give my love to Dr. Schmartz."

# The Art
## of
# Being a Patient

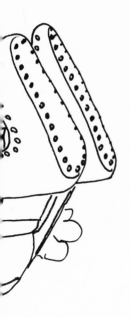

## ANSWERS

"Doctor! You must give me answers!"
    Silence filled the lonely room. . . .
"Does anxiety cause cancers?"
    Silence like an ancient tomb. . . .
"Doctor! This just isn't fair!"
    Silence hovered all around. . . .
"We're not getting anywhere!"
    Silence as if one were drowned. . . .
"Doctor! You are not so nice!"
    Silence like the darkest night. . . .
"I am paying for advice!"
    Silence everywhere in sight. . . .
"You're not skilled in psychic arts!"
    Silence like the world below. . . .
"And I'm telling Dr. Schmartz!"
    "What is it you want to know?"

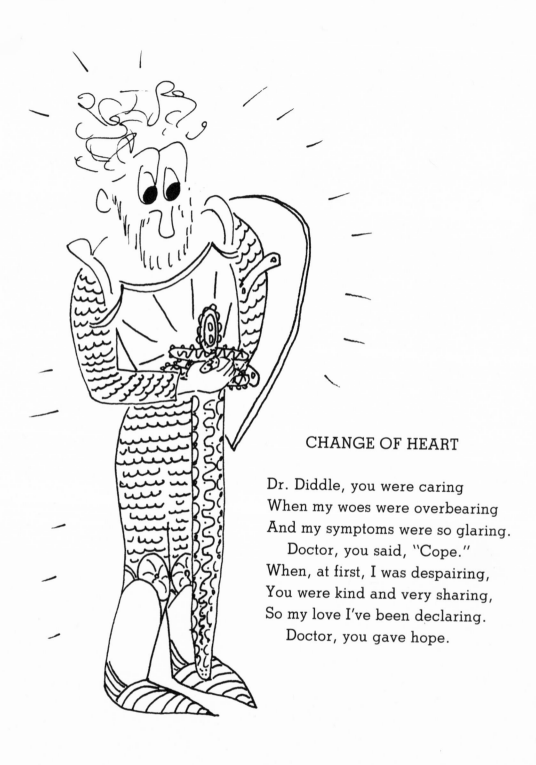

## CHANGE OF HEART

Dr. Diddle, you were caring
When my woes were overbearing
And my symptoms were so glaring.
    Doctor, you said, "Cope."
When, at first, I was despairing,
You were kind and very sharing,
So my love I've been declaring.
    Doctor, you gave hope.

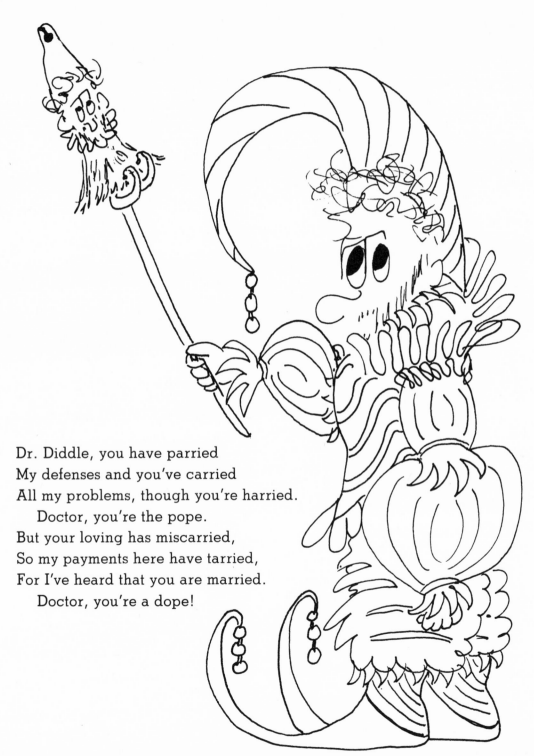

Dr. Diddle, you have parried
My defenses and you've carried
All my problems, though you're harried.
    Doctor, you're the pope.
But your loving has miscarried,
So my payments here have tarried,
For I've heard that you are married.
    Doctor, you're a dope!

# S'POSIN'

S'posin' the world comes to an end.
S'posin' I lose my only friend.
S'posin' the FBI should call.
S'posin' the sky begins to fall.
S'posin' I start to scream or sob.
S'posin' I'm fired from my job.
S'posin' I go out and I'm mugged.
S'posin' the drinking water's drugged.
S'posin' I spend my life in jail.
S'posin' my therapy should fail.
S'posin' I never have success.
S'posin' I can't find happiness.
S'posin' my whole life I am poor.
S'posin' the Russians start a war.
S'posin' I die before I'm thirty.
S'posin' I get . . . your carpet dirty!

# ADULTERY

"It was not 'adultery'?"
Asked the doctor, with a shrug.
    "It was not 'adultery,'"
    Grinned the patient, very smug.
"But it wasn't spin-the-bottle,"
Quipped the doctor, quite perplexed.
    "Well, I know I went full throttle;
    After all, I'm oversexed."
"But, why not 'adultery'?
You've a wife," the doctor parried.
    "*I'm* not single, I agree,
    But the *lady* wasn't married."

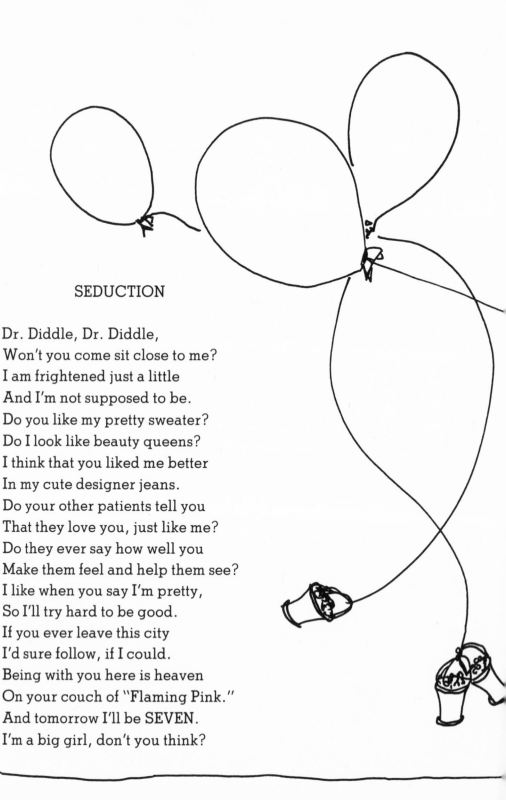

## SEDUCTION

Dr. Diddle, Dr. Diddle,
Won't you come sit close to me?
I am frightened just a little
And I'm not supposed to be.
Do you like my pretty sweater?
Do I look like beauty queens?
I think that you liked me better
In my cute designer jeans.
Do your other patients tell you
That they love you, just like me?
Do they ever say how well you
Make them feel and help them see?
I like when you say I'm pretty,
So I'll try hard to be good.
If you ever leave this city
I'd sure follow, if I could.
Being with you here is heaven
On your couch of "Flaming Pink."
And tomorrow I'll be SEVEN.
I'm a big girl, don't you think?

# MORE!

Dr. Diddle! Dr. Diddle!
It is certainly a riddle
That I see you far too little—
    Only twenty times a week.
And you show such deep abhorrence
Towards my asking for assurance
That it's trying my endurance
    So that I can hardly speak.

Dr. Diddle! Dr. Diddle!
I am really in a twiddle,
Maybe even paraniddle.
    You aren't seeing me enough.
Though I come for analyzin',
What I want is your advisin'.
All I get is criticizin'.
    Dr. Diddle, you're too tough!

# GUILT

Doc, I'm in an awful jam!
I busted out, I'm on the lam,
I'm taking dope, I'm selling drugs,
I'm dealing with a pack of thugs,
I kicked my mom and slugged my pop,
I robbed a bank and shot a cop,
I kidnapped some dumb wealthy dame
So's I could pay you when I came,
'Cause yesterday I felt some GUILT
Which made my calm insides go TILT!
And guilt feels bad, it wrecked my day.
You gotta make it go away!
'Cause if you don't, I'll wreck this place!
So, Doc . . . will you accept my case?

## CONFIDENTIALITY

"Dr. Diddle, it's essential
That you keep this confidential.
What I know has got potential
To be truly dynamite!"
    "Ah," smiled Diddle knowingly,
    "Confidentiality
Is our 'golden rule,' you see.
What you say will be airtight."

"I'm not certain I can trust you.
What I know may just disgust you.
And I fear you'll not adjust to
What I think should be revealed."
    "There is nothing you can tell me,"
    Soothed the doctor, "to repel me,
    Let alone destroy or fell me—
    And, of course, my lips are sealed."
"Well, your wife, who's very cute,
Was seen at the Institute
With this man of high repute. . . .
And they're having an affair!
I do not recall his title
But I hear he's very vital
And they say that every night he'll
Swagger off with her somewhere."
    Diddle shrieked, "My analyst
    And my wife met in a tryst?
    For my mill this is some grist!
    Oh, what troubles have begun!
    I can't tell him in our sessions.
    I can't ask her for confessions.
    I must sit on these transgressions. . . .
    Sigmund Freud—what have you done?"
"Doctor, have you lost your cool?
Conflict with your 'golden rule'?
I must tell you—*April Fool!*
You're so easy to hoodwink.
I just thought I'd have a spree
In my session, just to see
Confidentiality
Give a headache to my Shrink."

# TOO

Dr. Diddle, you're too young
To have psychiatric sense,
So I'm going to hold my tongue
Till you've more experience.

Dr. Diddle, you're too old
To know how I feel and think,
So my tale must go untold.
I should get a younger shrink.

Dr. Diddle, you're too straight
To grasp what I have to say.
I don't think I'd hesitate
If my therapist were gay.

Dr. Diddle, you're a male.
Women's feelings you can't know,
So my therapy must fail.
You can't comprehend my woe.

Diddle thought, It is my plight
Not to be a senile youth
Who's a gay hermaphrodite.
Then, by God, I'd hear the TRUTH!

136

## YOU

So you've not been analyzed?
I think you'll be quite surprised.
Dr. Diddle jots down notes
Of the very choicest quotes.
He's collected quite a few—
We've been analyzing YOU!

## THE KNOCKOUT IN THE GROUP

They all wanted to recoil
When new members joined the Group.
It was giving castor oil
When they longed for chicken soup.
Nancy Sue looked like a knockout
When she came there her first day,
But the members tried to block out
The event in every way.
"So what brings you to our party?"
Someone ruffled up some fur.
"You seem like a little smarty!"
Someone else was taunting her.
"This Group is too big already!"
Came another hostile voice.
"Nothing's stable! Nothing's steady!
No one gave us guys a choice!"
"I don't know if this new creep'll
Help us here—this Nancy Drew!"
"I don't think I like you people,
And my name is Nancy Sue!"

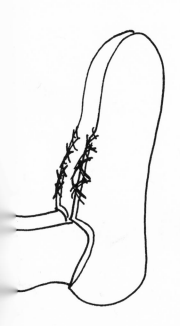

"It seems that the Group's scapegoating
The new member," Diddle said.
"All this rage you are emoting
You should vent at me instead."
He did not let them harangue her
As she sat there looking grim.
He identified their anger
And directed it towards him.
"Dr. Diddle, you're a dummy!"
Someone started the attack.
"And I think you are a rummy!
And you're nuts about your back!"
"Dr. Schmartz I have consulted,"
Voiced another. "He's some Shrink!
He is totally revolted
By your couch of 'Flaming Pink'!"
"Dr. Diddle, you're neurotic!
Sidewalks seem to you a tar pit.
Your obsessions's idiotic,
Such concern about your carpet!"
"Dr. Diddle, you're perverted!
You think porno shows are bliss.
And I've already alerted
Your Society of this."
Nancy Sue squealed, "This is super!
What a great Group I have found!"
Diddle sat there in a stupor—
KO'd in the second round.

## PIPE SCREAMS

Dr. Diddle, I've a gripe!
It's about your smelly pipe.
You just sit and puff away
Any time of night or day.
It's an uncouth thing to do,
And I'm trapped in here with you!
It's unhealthy smoke you blow.
As a doctor, you should know!
I have come here for a cure
But you're killing me for sure!
I'll get cancer of the lung,
You'll get cancer of the tongue.
Well, my session's over now.
You survived this one somehow,
Though you look half scared to death.
Next week . . . let's discuss your breath.

# FRIGID

Dr. Diddle, you're too rigid
To treat someone who is frigid.
You may be a keen observer
But that doesn't kindle fervor.
You may flash your M.D. shingle,
Still that doesn't make me tingle.
Your technique's too stale and rusty
To help me feel hot and lusty.
This process I'm undergoing
Doesn't start my juices flowing.
Therapy is disenchanting
When it comes to sexy panting.

What good are you doing me?
All I get is . . . therapy.

## TABOO

"But you can't!" cried Dr. Diddle.
"It would compromise our work."
  "Oh, I must," cajoled the patient,
  "For my needs drive me berserk."
"You must try," the doctor told her,
"To control your pressing needs."
  "That sounds awful," moaned the patient.
  "There's no fun where that course leads."
"It's a no-no!" warned the doctor.
"That's professional advice."
  "But I'm itching so," she panted,
  "To go off to paradise."
"But it isn't therapeutic!"
Diddle stressed emphatically.
  "It would feel so good," she murmured.
  "I'd have less anxiety."
"Sometimes patients choose to do it
When *I* want to," Diddle said.
  "If I wait till then," she whispered,
  "All my urges may be dead."
"I'll consent," the doctor yielded,
"Though it gives me trepidation."
  "Why," she sighed, "must it sound wicked
  Just to take a week's vacation?"

## MILIEU THERAPY

Dr. Diddle, here I sit.
I can't seem to think one bit.
My mind simply draws a blank,
No key to my memory bank.
In my bathroom thoughts just race.
That is my best thinking place.
I'm a wiz at higher math
While I'm soaking in my bath.
I can fantasize an hour
When I take a steaming shower.
All it takes for me to think
Is a bathtub and a sink.
That's where I can work the best. . . .
Doctor, I have one request:
Do you think we might resume
Treatment in your powder room?

## HYPOCHONDRIAC

Dr. Diddle, you're a quack!
I'm no hypochondriac!
You paint everything so black.
Your perspective's out of whack.
Sensitivity you lack.
Somehow you have lost the knack,
'Cause you're really off the track.
I don't need this kind of flak.
I'll give therapy the sack
If I find that you're a hack.
On your wall there is a plaque
Saying you're a crackerjack.
Of degrees you have a stack
And you're in the *Almanac*,
Yet you lay there and attack,
Labeling me "maniac."

*You* complain about your back.
*I'm* the hypochondriac?

## MASOCHIST

I was once a masochist.
Pain had me in its ugly grip,
For every lovely lass I kissed
I'd want to bite me on my lip.
It hurt me being masochistic.
That began to worry me.
Thought I'd be a mass statistic,
So I went for therapy.
My shrink, I think, was alchemistic,
For he sure transmuted me.
I have changed . . . I'm now sadistic.
Would you like a date with me?

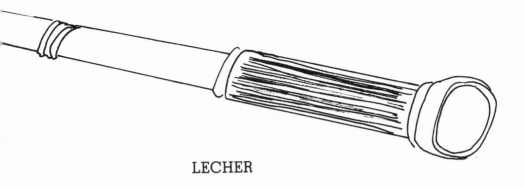

## LECHER

Dr. Diddle, you're a lecher!
Why, I even bet you get'cher
Kicks from hearing sexy tales
From fast dames and lusty males.
You hear with acuity
About my promiscuity.
If I mention "bra" or "garter,"
I observe you breathing harder.
If I speak of "underwear,"
You start squirming in your chair.
If I bring up "private parts,"
You start phoning Dr. Schmartz. . . .

Better keep your phone in view—
Have I got a tale for you!

## VAMPIRE

"You are of the living dead?"
Dr. Diddle gulped and said.
"And to Dracula you're wed?
Biting necks is what you dread?
It's horrendous to aspire
To a life as a vampire
When you're fearful to acquire
The one substance you desire.
Oh, this case is quite a beaut!
Something here does not compute.
I must call the Institute.
I know someone most astute."

Schmartz groused, "Why all this confusion?
Treat the lady for delusion.
If that proves the wrong conclusion—
Give the demon a transfusion."

## EXHIBITIONIST

I'm an exhibitionist.
Doc, I'll stop if you insist,
Though I often can't resist
    Making people yell.
There are questions you must ask
If my problems you'll unmask,
But before we start our task—
    Let's play SHOW AND TELL.

# SUPERZERO

"You're supposed to be a God,
Not an empty-headed clod!"
Diddle thought he'd need a bath,
Being spattered by the wrath
Of his patient spewing there,
Pounding loudly on his chair.
"I expect a SUPER-HERO,
Not a knuckle-headed Zero!
If my sanity's in danger,
Why aren't you the great Lone Ranger?
Who'll defeat the Master Plan
If you are not Superman?
I need Wonder Woman too—
Even Mighty Mouse will do!
All my demons we can't slaughter
If you cannot walk on water!
You just listen there and sulk.
Why won't you become the Hulk?
Or be Merlin with a wand!
Can't you even be James Bond?
To protect the innocent
You must not be impotent!
Eat your spinach! Be a Popeye!
Be the psychiatric Top Guy!
Just the Lord of Psychic Arts—
Oh, why aren't you Dr. Schmartz?"

## KLEPTOMANIAC

What you steal you don't give back.
Moral judgment you must lack.
You're a kleptomaniac
And you're not a common crook.
They're compulsive acts you do.
You don't need what you accrue.
Let's just find an hour for you.
Hey, where's my appointment book?

## PROSTITUTE

Doctor, I'm a prostitute,
Just a lass of disrepute.
For love I don't give a hoot,
    So my problem's real.
Tell me, Doctor, what's your fee?
That's amazing as can be.
You charge just the same as me!
    Say, let's make a deal. . . .

## THE PUZZLE OF HER LIFE

Dr. Diddle, I adore you.
Won't you come sit next to me?
I have got this yearning for you,
But it's not just "sex" to me.
Come and share this lovely couch.
Would that seem too gross to you?
For your honor I would vouch.
I need to be close to you.
Dr. Diddle, you're so shy,
That's why you're not acquiescing.
I'm just asking you to lie
Next to me without undressing.
Maybe you think this sounds corny
But I'm certain it would cure me.
It's not that I'm feeling horny,
It would greatly reassure me.
I feel that you're much too distant
Sitting there so far away.
Could it be I'm too insistent?
Could it be that you are gay?
All my strengths you could unfetter
And it's bound to set me free.
Your technique would work much better
Talking horizontally.
I don't know why you refuse this,
It's the puzzle of my life.
As a patient, I'd excuse this—
But, my dear, I am your wife!

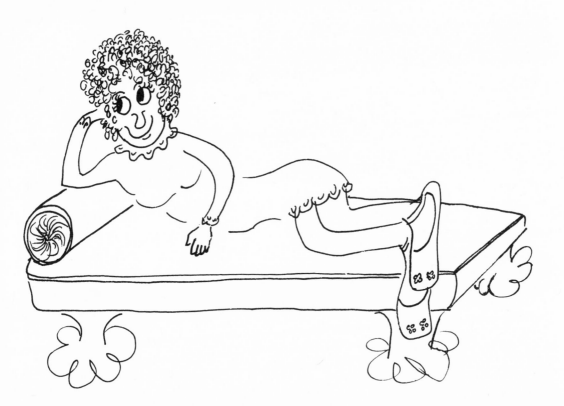

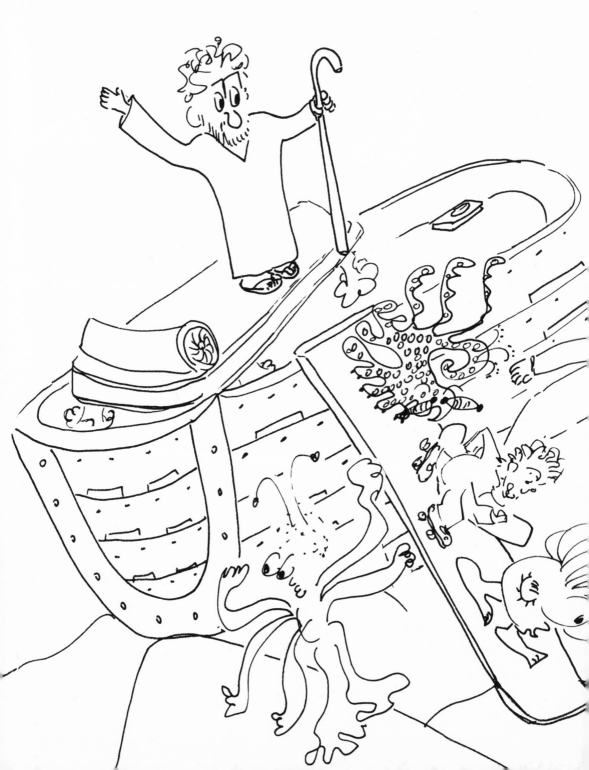

# The Art
# of
# Terminating Therapy

## JUST NIBBLING

"I'm too fat," the patient moaned.
As she spoke, the chair legs groaned.
"I'm all flabby, nothing's toned.
   What am I to do?
I should surely be a winner
Skipping breakfast, lunch and dinner,
Yet I don't get any thinner,
   So I've come to you."
"This is quite a weighty matter,"
Sighed the doctor. "You'll get fatter
Sitting here with that huge platter,
   Eating every sweet."
"Doctor, I resent your quibbling!
I'm afraid our time you're fribbling.
I'm not eating, I'm just nibbling.
   I deserve a **TREAT**!"
"Maybe **TREAT**ment you deserve.
Please put down that gross hors d'oeuvre.
Therapy is what I serve.
   It won't make you stout."
"Therapy is not too tasty!"
Snapped the woman. "I've been hasty.
It does not compare with pastry!"
   And she waddled out.

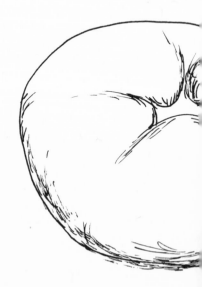

## MARITAL THERAPY

### FIRST SESSION

He said, "Hot."
She said, "Cold."
She said, "Young."
He said, "Old."
He said, "Bought."
She said, "Sold."
She said, "Meek."
He said, "Bold."
He said, "Lead."
She said, "Gold."
She said, "Drop."
He said, "Hold."
He said, "Praise."
She said, "Scold."
She said, "Asked."
He said, "Told."
He said, "Open."
She said, "Fold."
She said, "Break."
He said, "Mold."
They said, "Guilty?"
Diddle said, "Paroled."

# FINAL SESSION

He said, "Hot."
She said, "True."
She said, "Young."
He said, "You."
He said, "Love."
She said, "Coo."
She said, "Us."
He said, "Glue."
He said, "Fights."
She said, "Few."
She said, "Cherish."
He said, "Woo."
He said, "Touch."
She said, "Do."
She said, "Thrived."
He said, "Grew."
He said, "Kitten."
She said, "Mew."
She said, "Joy."
He said, "Anew."
They said, "Thanks."
Diddle said, "Phew!"

## FAMILY SESSION

"I don't like the dumb expression
Junior's wearing on his face!
This is our first Family Session,"
Father griped. "It's a disgrace!"
"Oh, you leave my son alone!"
Mother shouted on the spot.
"Should he sit there like a stone
Or look happy when he's not?"
"Don't you use that tone with me!"
Bellowed Father at his wife.
"All you do is disagree!
You're a blight upon my life!"
"Tell us, Junior," Diddle said,
"What you think of all of that."
Junior shook his little head,
"Well, I think it's tit for tat."
"Very good," smiled Dr. Diddle.
"Can you tell us something more?"
Junior offered, "They're a little
Like my buddies playing War.
Dad's supposed to be a grownup
But behaves just like a kid.
And I've never heard him own up
To some awful things he did.
Mommy's not too good at mothering
But she doesn't want to know.
I think she is much too smothering
And that doesn't let me grow."

"This kid's got some sense of humor!
I could tear him limb from limb!"
Growled the father. "There's a rumor,
Diddle, that you're coaching him!"
"Yes!" screamed Mother. "He talks funny.
All those fancy words, oh, brother!
I'm not paying you good money
To turn him against his mother!
Let's go, Junior, come with me!
This old doctor is a fool!
You can learn psychology
From nice teachers at your school!"
"I don't like the dumb expression
Diddle's wearing on his face!
This is our last Family Session!"
Father roared. "It's a disgrace!"

## IN THE DOGHOUSE

Dr. Diddle, Dr. Diddle,
I am in a fit of pique!
I'm bewildered by the riddle
Of your alien technique.
When I came last week to see you
For my nasty facial tic,
You claimed, "I know how to free you
And my method works real quick."
Well, I won't pay you one dollar
And I don't care what you think!
If I wear this old tick collar
I would *really* need a shrink!

## GOING, GOING . . .

Doctor, I am terminating!
You may have a sermon waiting,
But this plan's been germinating
For at least an hour I'd say.
You may label this resistance
And think that I want some distance,
But I don't need your assistance.
I got better yesterday!

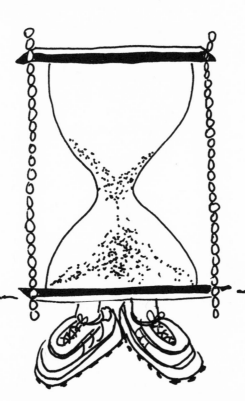

## TOO SLOW

After all this time, it's ending.
No more therapy with you.
All the effort I've been spending
Taking risks and working through.
Analyzing my neurosis
Was a monumental task.
Then we found it was psychosis
That my symptoms tried to mask.
I remember how it started,
All the acting out I did.
How you gradually imparted
Knowledge of my violent id.
Gone, my crushing superego!
Gone, my overwhelming guilt!
From strict toilet training, we know.
Analyzed that to the hilt!
My poor ego was deficient
And I tended to distort,
But your efforts were sufficient
I am happy to report.
You assured me I'd get stronger
And that someday down the line
I would need your help no longer
And that I would function fine.
Well, my only criticizing
Is that treatment was so slow,
For we started analyzing
Almost SEVEN WEEKS ago!

## BESTED

Doctor, you are such a wonder!
You don't make a single blunder.
You knock all distress asunder.
    Doctor, you're the BEST!
Though I'm leaving, I admire
All the strength that you inspire.
From your help I'll now retire.
    Oh, I've just joined EST.

## DIDDLE-ATION

On the couch she grinned away,
Looking titillated.
"Doctor, you have made my day—
I've been 'Diddle-ated'!"

## IN A NUTSHELL

"Doctor! What big eyes you have!"
   "That's transference," said the Shrink.
"Doctor! What big spies you have!"
   "That's delusion, don't you think?"
"Doctor! What big bills you have!"
   "That's resistance," he assured.
"Doctor! What big skills you have!"
   "That's reality— You're cured!"

To our dear friend and cherished critic, Lois P. Sheinfeld, our thanks for her thoughtful comments and careful reading of our manuscript, her support and encouragement, her frowns and laughter throughout our work on this book. . . .

To our patients, our gratitude for teaching us so much about the art of shrinking. . . .

*Jerry Klinman*

*Cynthia S. Klinman*

JEROME J. KLINMAN, the author, is a graduate of Haverford College, Jefferson Medical College, and the psychiatric residency program of the Institute of Living in Hartford. A Diplomate of the American Board of Psychiatry and Neurology, Dr. Klinman has supervised psychiatric residents at the Institute of Living and at New York Medical College, and was Chief of the Psychiatric Outpatient Department at Valley Forge General Hospital. He has a private practice in psychiatry in Manhattan.

CYNTHIA S. KLINMAN, the illustrator, received her bachelor's and master's degrees from Bryn Mawr College, her doctorate from the University of Connecticut, and is a graduate of the William Alanson White Institute of Psychoanalysis in New York. She has published scientific articles, taught undergraduate and graduate students in psychology, and has served as Chief Psychologist of the Philadelphia Psychiatric Center, Director of Psychological Services at the Institute of the Pennsylvania Hospital, and Director of the Psychiatric Day Hospital at Roosevelt Hospital in New York. She has a private practice in psychoanalysis and psychotherapy in Manhattan.

The Klinmans, who have been practicing the art of shrinking for over twenty years, live in New York City with their daughters. This is their first book.